DINOSAURS
OF AUSTRALIA

Australian Geographic 3D

First published in 2015 by:
Bauer Media
54 Park Street, Sydney, NSW 2000
Telephone: (02) 9263 9813
Fax: (02) 9216 3731
Email: editorial@ausgeo.com.au
www.australiangeographic.com.au

Australian Geographic customer service:
1300 555 176 (local call rate within Australia).
From overseas +61 2 8667 5295

Australian Geographic

Book editor Lauren Smith
Text Wes Judd, John Pickrell, Lauren Smith
Illustrations Lida Xing and Yujiang Han
Book design Filip Bartkowiak
Picture research Jess Teideman
Print production Chris Clear
Sub-editor John Pickrell
Proof reader Ken Eastwood
Interactive Producers - 3D
Apattra Hongsuwong, Mark Jamais
Interactive Designer Daniel DiPaola
Managing Director Matthew Stanton
Publishing Director – Specialist Division
Brendon Hill
Publisher Jo Runciman
Editor-in-Chief, Australian Geographic
Chrissie Goldrick

Created with support from:
viewa
Eye Candy Animation
Western Australian Museum

Printed in China by C & C Offset Printing Co. Ltd.

Cover:
Dinosaur Models: Lida Xing and Yujiang Han;
Theropod Tooth: Australian Opal Centre/Robert Smith
Trace Fossil: Phil Hill/Getty
Opalised Fossil: Steve Morton/Museum Victoria

Bring these dinosaurs back from the dead!

Use a tablet or smartphone to discover 3D dinos, bonus interactive features and videos.

STEP 1

Download the free ***viewa*** app from the App Store or Google play.

STEP 2

Scan the page whenever you see this ***viewa*** logo to get up close and personal with these ancient creatures.

MORE HANDS-ON FUN!

Scan this page for even more extras.

Create your own dinosaurs!

Take a picture with the dinos in our photobooth!

Learn how to pronounce their names!

Download wallpapers for your smartphone or tablet!

CONTENTS

Though they did live at the same time, flying and marine reptiles are not actually dinosaurs.

What is a DINOSAUR?

With every fossil found, we're learning more and more about dinosaurs.

STAMPEDE!

Scan this page to see these dinosaurs run.

The word dinosaur actually means "terrible lizard'!

DINO DETAILS

Dinosaurs are land-based reptiles that lived between 227 and 66 million years ago. One of the factors that we use to define them is that they hold their limbs straight beneath them, rather than out to their sides like crocodiles.

There are two main groups of dinosaurs. There are the saurischian, or 'lizard-hipped' dinosaurs, that included the giant long-necked sauropods (such as *Diamantinasaurus*) and all the two-legged, **carnivorous** theropods (such as *Tyrannosaurus* and *Australovenator*).

The other group are the ornithischian or 'bird-hipped' dinosaurs which included frilled and armoured species (such as *Triceratops* and *Minmi*) and herd-living herbivores (such as *Muttaburrasaurus*).

Technically, dinosaurs are all animals descended from the last shared ancestor of the ornithischians and saurischians – and that means that all birds, even the ones we know today, are actually dinosaurs!

The famous *Triceratops* was a kind of ornithischian, but so far we haven't found any evidence of *Triceratops* living in Australia.

What is a FOSSIL?

Fossils are the prehistoric remains of animals or plants from a long time ago.

There are two types of fossils. Body fossils, which look like parts of skeletons, are the fossils of bones that got covered up by mud or sand. Most of the time, minerals seep into the bones, slowly replacing the bone but keeping the shape as mud and sand harden into rock around it.

The rock protects the fossil, and when palaeontologists find it they very carefully dig it out of the dirt. They can break easily, so the scientists have to be very gentle.

Sometimes, fossils have been preserved in ice, such as the mammoths found in Alaska, or in tar pits, like the one found in Los Angeles, California.

The second kind of fossil is a trace fossil. This is where there's a sign of animal activity that's been preserved, like the dinosaur footprints at Lark Quarry in Queensland. So far, the oldest known Australian dinosaur only dates back 170 million years, but scientists have found tracks near Dinmore in Queensland that date back 220 million years!

Australian dinosaur body fossils are often only fragments or pieces, such as these two. On the the left is part of the spine of a ornithopod and below is the tooth of a theropod.

Australian palaeontologist Steve Salisbury at work in Broome, WA.

3D

KEEP DIGGING!

Scan this page and tap away the rocks to reveal the fossil. Then tap on the skeleton to see it come alive.

FOSSIL FIND

When palaeontologists find fossils, they study them to identify which parts belong together. Even though they don't usually find a complete skeleton, they're often able to put together an idea of what the dinosaur looked like. They'll study similar dinosaurs, or even look at modern animals that have a similar bone structure, and use that to develop an idea of what the whole skeleton looked like.

One of the exciting things about studying dinosaurs is that every time we find new fossils, we're able to improve our understanding of what dinosaurs looked like, and how they lived!

Ozraptor subotaii

AGE: Mid Jurassic (170 million years old)

LENGTH: 3 metres	**HEIGHT:** 1 metre	**WEIGHT:** 100kg

REGION: Western Australia	**DIET:** Carnivore

In 1966 a shin bone was found by four twelve-year-old schoolboys near Geraldton, in Western Australia. When a model of the bone was sent to England, experts first suspected that the bone belonged to a turtle! *Ozraptor* is now thought to have been a speedy meat-eater.

Of all of the Australian dinosaurs discovered so far, Ozraptor is the oldest.

The partial shin bone found in 1966 is still the only fossil evidence we have for this dinosaur.

FACT: The *Ozraptor* part of the name is pretty clear, but *Subotaii* is based on a character from the *'Conan the Barbarian'* movies – Subotai was a quick little thief.

FACT: It wasn't until 1998 that they decided the fossil was from a dinosaur instead of a turtle – more than thirty years after discovery!

HOW TO SAY IT: oz-rap-tor

Australovenator wintonensis

AGE: Mid Cretaceous (93 million years old)

LENGTH: 6 metres	HEIGHT: 2 metres	WEIGHT: 300-400kg

REGION: Queensland	DIET: Carnivore

This speedy dinosaur had huge claws on its hands and slender-toed feet, and has been described as the cheetah of Cretaceous Australia. We've found the most complete fossil of this species compared to all of the other Australian carnivorous dinosaurs. It was discovered in 2009 by palaeontologist Scott Hocknull near Winton, Queensland.

ACTUAL SIZE!

3D

WATCH OUT!

Scan this page to come face-to-face with this carnivore!

These two dinosaurs look different, but they're both *Australovenator*! Every illustrator has a unique idea about the appearance of a dinosaur, and so our 3D models and illustrations might look a little different!

FACT: The fossil skeleton that was discovered of *Australovenator* is nicknamed 'Banjo' after the famous Australian bush poet Banjo Paterson.	**FACT:** The name *Australovenator* comes from two Latin words – 'australis' meaning 'south', and 'venator', which means 'hunter'. So *Australovenator* means 'southern hunter'.

HOW TO SAY IT: aus-tra-low-ven-ah-tor

Activation & Inset: Eye Candy

Australovenator was a swift predator, and in this illustration, can be seen making short work of a young *Diamantinasaurus*.

When did Australia's dinosaurs EXIST?

Dinosaurs lived between 227 and 66 million years ago, but they didn't all live at once.

mya = million years ago

Dinosaurs were the dominant group of land animals during the Triassic, Jurassic and Cretaceous periods. Most of the known Australian dinosaurs are from the Cretaceous period.

TRIASSIC PERIOD (248–213 mya)

248 mya → 213 mya

227 mya
First dinosaurs

225 mya
First mammals

JURASSIC PERIOD (213–144mya)

213 mya → 144 mya

170 – 168 mya
Ozraptor subotaii

167 – 165 mya
Rhoetosaurus brownei

160 mya
Oldest flowering plant and bird fossils

CRETACEOUS PERIOD (144–66mya)

144 mya → 66 mya

144 – 125 mya
Minmi

125 – 113 mya
Kakuru

125 – 120 mya
Qantassaurus

125 mya
Oldest marsupial fossils

112 – 106 mya
Fulgurotherium

110 – 106 mya
Atlascopcosaurus
Leaellynasaura
Timimus

105 – 101 mya
Austrosaurus
Muttaburrasaurus

94.5 – 92 mya
Australovenator
Diamantinasaurus
Wintonotitan

Australia was a very different place during this time. Australia was once part of a southern **supercontinent** called Gondwana, which slowly shifted and divided over millions of years.

CENOZOIC PERIOD (66mya – today)

66 mya → TODAY

66 mya
Extinction of non-bird dinosaurs

52 mya
Oldest gum tree fossils

28 mya
First kangaroos

200,000 years ago
First modern humans

Atlascopcosaurus loadsi

AGE: Early Cretaceous (110 million years old)		
LENGTH: 3 metres	**HEIGHT:** 1 metre	**WEIGHT:** 20kg
REGION: Victoria	**DIET:** Herbivore	

Only a few bones from the head of this dinosaur have been discovered, back in 1989, but it's enough to reveal that it was a member of the ornithopods – a group of two-legged herbivores. Most feathered species found so far have been carnivorous dinosaurs, but there are a few hints that herbivores like *Atlascopcosaurus* may have been feathered as well.

One of the *Atlascopcosaurus* fossils we've found is a jawbone.

Atlas Copco is the company that sponsored the dig where the fossils were first found.

FACT: *Atlascopcosaurus* was found at Dinosaur Cove in Victoria, by Patricia Vickers-Rich and Tom Rich. They also found *Serendipaceratops* and *Timimus*.

HOW TO SAY IT: at-lass-cop-coe-sore-us

Minmi paravertebra

AGE: Early Cretaceous (140 million years old)		
LENGTH: 3 metres	**HEIGHT:** 1 metre	**WEIGHT:** 100kg
REGION: Queensland		**DIET:** Herbivore

***Minmi* had tough skin. This dinosaur even had armour on its belly!**

HEAPS TOUGH 3D

viewa

Scan this page to see a 3D *Minmi*!

When some remains of this stocky species were first found in the 1960s, it was instantly recognised as an armoured anklyosaur type of dinosaur. In 1990, scientists unearthed an almost complete skeleton in north-western Queensland. There were even impressions of its skin and the leftover contents of its stomach!

FACT: When they studied the contents of the stomach, they found that it ate seeds and fruit from flowering plants, as well as ferns.

FACT: It seems that after the *Minmi* died, it got washed out to sea. Millions of years later, the sea was gone and the fossil was hidden until someone noticed a rock that looked a bit like an anklebone in 1990!

HOW TO SAY IT: min-my

How are all the dinosaurs RELATED?

Ozraptor **and *Minmi* might not look alike, but they both have a place on the family tree.**

Australia's dinosaurs come from many different branches of the family tree and are related to famous species from other parts of the world!

3D

MEET THE FAMILY

Scan this page for an interactive dinosaur family photo album!

viewa

KEY

Dinosaur group
Family characteristics
Examples of group members
Coloured names indicate Australian species

DINOSAURS

Ornithischians
(bird-hipped dinosaurs)

Ornithopods
Bipedal herbivores, such as: *Hypsilophodon, Parasaurolophus, Muttaburrasaurus, Leaellynasaura, Qantassaurus, Atlascopcosaurus*

Pachycephalosaurs
Dome-headed, **bipedal** dinosaurs, such as: *Pachycephalasaurus Stegoceras*

Ceratopsians
Quadrupedal frilled and horned dinosaurs, such as: *Triceratops, Centrosaurus, Serendipaceratops*

Thyreophorans
(armoured dinosaurs)

Stegosaurs
Quadrupedal herbivores with plates and spikes, such as: *Stegosaurus*

Ankylosaurs
Low-slung, armoured dinosaurs, such as: *Ankylosaurus, Minmi*

Saurischians
(lizard-hipped dinosaurs)

Sauropods
Massive, long-necked, **quadrupedal** dinosaurs, such as: *Brachiosaurus, Diplodocus Diamantinasaurus, Austrosaurus, Rhoetosaurus, Wintonotitan*

Theropods
(bipedal carnivores)

Ceratosaurs
Predatory dinosaurs, such as: *Ceratosaurus, Ozraptor*

Carnosaurs
Ferocious predatory dinosaurs such as: *Allosaurus, Australovenator*

Tyrannosaurs
Predatory dinosaurs with powerful jaws, such as: *Tyrannosaurus, Timimus*

Dromaeosaurs
Lightly-built, speedy predators with feathers, such as: *Velociraptor, Microraptor*

Aves
Modern birds, capable of powered flight, such as: Eagle, cockatoo

Leaellynasaura amicagraphica

AGE: Early Cretaceous (110 million years old)

LENGTH: 1.5 metres	**HEIGHT:** 0.6 metres	**WEIGHT:** 10kg

REGION: Victoria	**DIET:** Herbivore

Its tail could be up to three times longer than the rest of its body.

3D

SAY HELLO

Scan this page to interact with a *Leaellynasaura*.

Leaellynasaura is a species that some experts now think might have been feathered!

This small plant-eater lived in the south of Australia when it was partly within the Antarctic Circle. The skull that was found, in Dinosaur Cove in Victoria, shows that it had a large brain, and large eyes that helped it keep watch for predators as it looked for food in the dark of the long Antarctic winter.

FACT: In the Antarctic winter, there would have been a four month stretch without any sunlight!	**FACT:** It was discovered by Patricia Vickers-Rich and Tom Rich, and named after their daughter Leaellyn.

HOW TO SAY IT: lee-allin-ah-sore-ah

Qantassaurus intrepidus

AGE: Early Cretaceous (120 million years old)

LENGTH: 1.5 metres | **HEIGHT:** 0.7 metres | **WEIGHT:** 45kg

REGION: Victoria | **DIET:** Herbivore

This species had large eyes compared with most dinosaurs, which would have helped it see better during the night.

Qantassaurus is a small dinosaur, about the size of a kangaroo, that was also discovered by Patricia Vickers-Rich and Tom Rich in Inverloch, Victoria in 1994. This dinosaur was a herbivore, and survived the cold environment by using its muscular cheeks and grinding teeth to eat a wide range of low-growing plants such as ferns.

FACT: *Qantassaurus* is the only dinosaur named after an airline – Qantas sponsored the dig on which the fossils of the species were found.

FACT: The long tail of the *Qantassaurus* would have helped it to turn quickly while it was running.

HOW TO SAY IT: kwant-uh-sore-us

The *Sinosauropteryx* fossil below was one of the first feathered dinosaurs analysed and experts discovered that it was ginger coloured, with a striped tail!

COLOURING IN

Some of the fossils that have been discovered recently have feathers! These feathered fossils mean that we're finally able to find out what colour some of the dinosaurs were. The colour of a feather, or the colour of your hair, is determined by the keratin inside it. Keratin is an incredibly tough **protein** that can survive for hundred of millions of years in fossils. By studying the feathers under a high-powered microscope, you can make out different types of pigment that determine particular colours.

Since the discovery of the first feathered dinosaur in 1996, scientists have started to consider that other dinosaurs, may have also had feathers.

THEY'RE SO FLUFFY!

Scan this page to see what a feather-covered *Timimus* would look like.

What did dinosaurs LOOK LIKE?

Did dinosaurs have scaly skin or feathers? Were they brightly coloured, or dull and drab? We're still learning the answers to both of these questions!

It's always been a bit of a mystery what colour the dinosaurs were! Even in instances where an impression of dinosaur skin has been found (usually a scaly, or pebbly texture) we have no way of knowing what colour they were!

Some palaeontologists say that dinosaur skin would have been a dull colour to help them blend in to their environment. If you think about the big land animals that exist today, like elephants, rhinoceroses and hippos, they're usually a drab grey or brown.

There are other palaeontologists though, who think that dinosaurs would have been brightly coloured, with purple, orange, red or blue skin! They suggest that, like birds, these different colours would have helped them identify one another and even help them find mates.

Timimus hermani

AGE: Early Cretaceous (105 million years old)		
LENGTH: 9 metres	**HEIGHT:** 3 metres	**WEIGHT:** 4 tonnes
REGION: Victoria	**DIET:** Herbivore	

When the fossils were first discovered in Dinosaur Cove in Victoria in 1994, scientists thought it was related to a group of herbivorous dinosaurs called ornithomimosaurs or 'bird-mimic lizards', which was a group of dinosaurs that looked a bit like ostriches. Scientists now think that *Timimus* is actually a distant relative of *Tyrannosaurus rex*!

Timimus would have been one of the faster dinosaurs, with long, strong legs.

This species is known only from two fossils of thighbones, one from an adult, and one from a juvenile *Timimus*.

FACT: *Timimus* was discovered by Patricia Vickers-Rich and Tom Rich, and they named it after their son, Tim.

FACT: Where *Timimus* was running around, it would have been very cold and dark in winter, and it's believed that this dinosaur hibernated through the cold seasons.

HOW TO SAY IT: tim-my-mus

Muttaburrasaurus langdoni

AGE: Early Cretaceous (105 million years old)

LENGTH: 9 metres | **HEIGHT:** 3 metres | **WEIGHT:** 4 tonnes

REGION: Queensland & New South Wales | **DIET:** Herbivore

The unusual bulge on its snout may have contained an inflatable air sac. This might have helped it make loud calls to other dinosaurs.

Muttaburrasaurus is our largest ornithopod, and we've found fossils from the species in both Queensland and New South Wales, including two skulls! This powerful herbivore could rear up on its back legs to reach tall trees and also to intimidate predators, though it sometimes moved on all four legs.

A replica skeleton model of *Muttaburrasaurus.*

FACT: It is named *Muttaburrasaurus* after the town in Queensland where it was first found – Muttaburra.

FACT: One of the skull fossils found in Queensland, at Dunluce Station, was used as a doorstop by the family that owned the station before they realised what it was!

HOW TO SAY IT: muta-burra-sore-us

Just how BIG were Australia's dinosaurs?

Some would have towered over you, and others would only come up to your knees.

SIZING UP

Scale:
1cm = 1m

Australia's largest known dinosaur was the *Rhoetosaurus*. The smallest known avian dinosaur is the weebill, a tiny songbird found across Australia today. The smallest known non-avian dinosaur was the *Leaellynasaura*, which only weighed 10kg – about as much as you did when you were a year old!

i *Rhoetosaurus* was our largest dinosaur, but a female blue whale would be almost double the length and more than nine times heavier – weighing in at 200 tonnes!

i The weebill weighs only six grams – about the weight of a ten cent coin.

THEY'RE ALIVE!

Scan this page then slowly move your phone around the room to see life-sized versions of these dinosaurs, plus scan the opposite page for a little surprise.

Rhoetosaurus brownei

AGE: Mid Jurassic (167 million years old)		
LENGTH: 18 metres	**HEIGHT:** 7 metres	**WEIGHT:** 20 tonnes
REGION: Queensland	**DIET:** Herbivore	

At 20 tonnes, a ***Rhoetosaurus*** would weigh as much as four elephants!

The first fossils of *Rhoetosaurus* were found in 1924 in Roma, Queensland, and more of the same skeleton was uncovered in 1976. It is named after the mythical Greek giant Rhoetos, and would have used its long neck to reach up to plants like **conifers.** *Rhoetosaurus* would have been a fairly slow mover, only capable of moving at about 15 km per hour, though it might not have moved around too much in a day.

This is a cast of a *Rhoetosaurus* femur – that's its thigh bone!

FACT: This was the first big dinosaur to be found in Australia, and the **stockmen** who found it first thought it was the remains of an escaped circus elephant!

HOW TO SAY IT: ree-toe-sore-us

Diamantinasaurus matildae

AGE: Mid Cretaceous (94 million years old)

LENGTH: 15 metres	**HEIGHT:** 5 metres	**WEIGHT:** 15 tonnes
REGION: Queensland	**DIET:** Herbivore	

This stocky-legged, broad-hipped dinosaur is one of the most complete Australian dinosaur skeletons. A heavy plant-eater with a long neck and tail, the region that the *Diamantinasaurus* would have lived in was a lush temperate area, with lots of billabongs, lakes and a variety of plants. The fossils were even found in what turned out to be a 94 million-year-old billabong.

PIECE IT TOGETHER

Scan this page to see how the skeleton of *Diamantinasaurus* was put together.

FACT: *Diamantinasaurus* is a sauropod (a large, **herbivorous**, four-legged dinosaur) and so is *Austrosaurus*, *Rhoetosaurus* and *Wintonotitan*.

FACT: The skeleton is nicknamed 'Matilda', after Banjo Paterson's famous ballad, which was written in 1885 near Winton, not too far from where these fossils were found.

HOW TO SAY IT: die-ah-man-teen-ah-sore-us

Where have we FOUND Australia's dinosaurs?

Dinosaur fossils and tracks have been found all over Australia! Where's the closest spot to you?

The dinosaur footprints found in Broome, Western Australia, are about 130 million years old!

In Broome, there's an 80km dinosaur trackway, where you can see the tracks of different types of dinosaurs, such as sauropods, stegosaurs and theropods!

MAKING AN IMPRESSION

viewa

Scan this page for a video about the Lark Quarry footprints.

There are over 3300 dinosaur tracks at Lark Quarry in Winton! They date back 95 million years, and for a long time scientists thought that it was the record of dinosaur stampede! Scientists now suspect that the footprints were left by dinosaurs crossing a river.

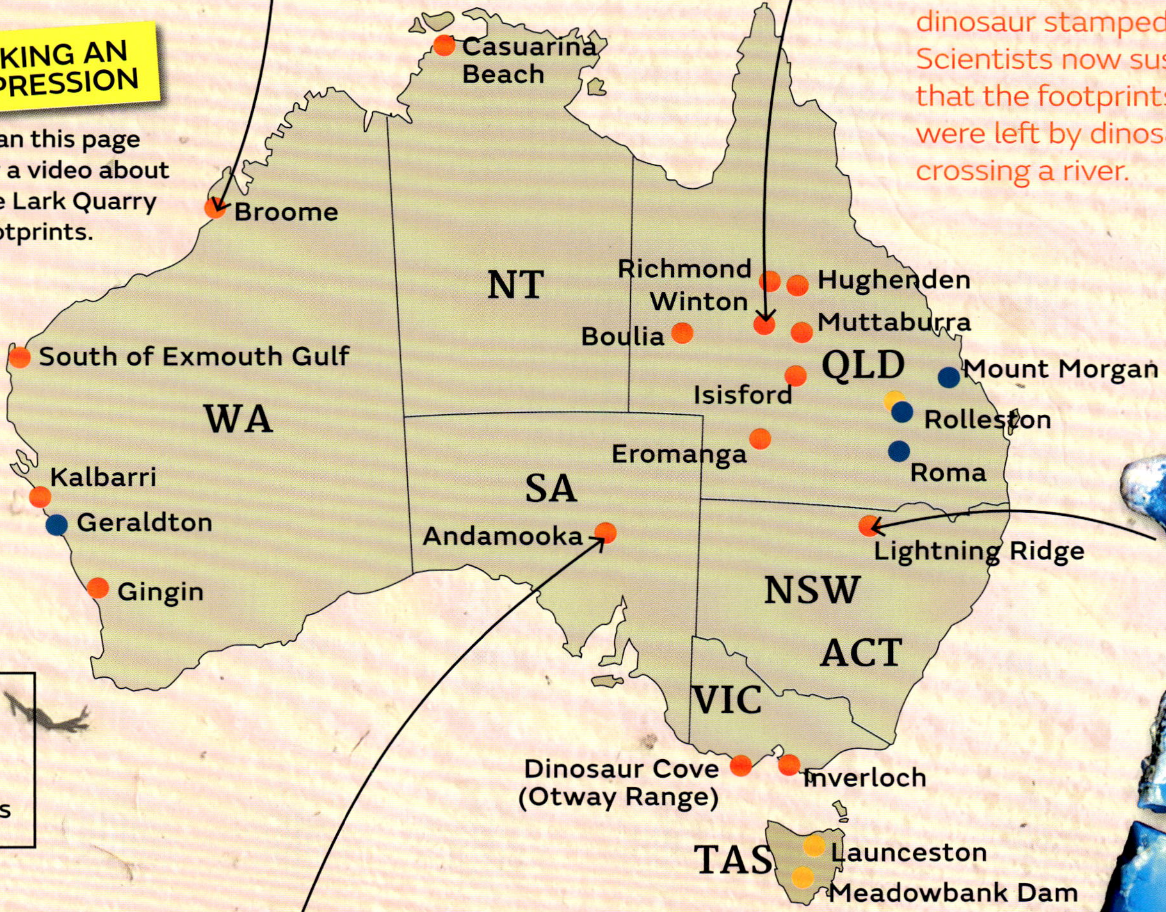

KEY

- Triassic
- Jurassic
- Cretaceous

At Andamooka, a shin bone was discovered that belonged to a small dinosaur called *Kakuru kujani*. We don't know much about this dinosaur yet, but hopefully we'll find more fossils for it soon so that we can understand it better!

The fossils found in Lightning Ridge are very special – they're made of opals, like this one from the dinosaur *Fulgurotherium australe*.

Wintonotitan wattsi

AGE: Mid Cretaceous (94.5 million years old)

LENGTH: 18 metres	**HEIGHT:** 5 metres	**WEIGHT:** 18 tonnes

REGION: Queensland	**DIET:** Herbivore

The first fossil of this towering plant-eater was first thought to belong to *Austrosaurus*. It was re-examined a few times in the 2000s and researchers finally declared it a unique species, making it the fourth Australian sauropod. It is nicknamed 'Clancy' after Banjo Paterson's ballad *Clancy of the Overflow* – it was also found near Winton not far from *Australovenator* and *Diamantinasaurus*.

This print in the ground at Broome shows the size and impact that a sauropod's footstep could have!

FACT: *Wintonotitan* is a kind of titanosaur – a group of sauropods that were the largest animals to ever walk on the planet.

FACT: The dinosaur tracks at Broome, Western Australia, tell us that Australia used to have even bigger dinosaurs than *Wintonotitan* and even *Austrosaurus* – they've found footsteps that are longer than 1.5m across!

HOW TO SAY IT: win-ton-oh-tie-tan

Austrosaurus mckillopi

AGE: Early Cretaceous (105 million years old)

LENGTH: 20 metres | **HEIGHT:** 5 metres | **WEIGHT:** 15 tonnes

REGION: Queensland | **DIET:** Herbivore

Discovered in north-central Queensland 80 years ago, *Austrosaurus* was our first known sauropod from the Cretaceous era. This long-necked species was able to reach tall trees and foliage.

Austrosaurus would have been about the same height as an adult giraffe!

Scientists now think that sauropods such as *Austrosaurus* would have actually avoided swampy areas, as it would have been difficult for these heavy animals to get around.

FACT: Scientists once thought that *Austrosaurus* spent a lot of time in the water, since it was found in an area with lots of plesiosaurs (a type of marine reptile). We know now that's not correct, however, and that it was a land-based animal.

FACT: *Austrosaurus* means 'southern reptile', and *mckillopi* refers to the McKillop brothers, who ran the farm where the fossils were found.

HOW TO SAY IT: aus-tro-sore-us

Are there any dinosaurs around TODAY?

Dinosaurs died out 66 million years ago, but there are animals alive today that bear an uncanny similarity to creatures that lived alongside those fearsome reptiles.

If you consider that birds are avian dinosaurs, there's actually a lot of dinosaurs alive today. There are around ten thousand species of birds in the world! Outside of birds, there are no true dinosaurs left alive.

Australia does have a few species, though, that look similar to species that existed in the same era as some of the dinosaurs.

Sarcosuchus is an extinct reptile and a distant relative of today's crocodiles. It lived around 112 million years ago and grew over 12 metres in length, making it the largest crocodilian to have ever lived.

Crocodiles aren't dinosaurs, but archosaurs. We know from fossil records that the first crocodilians appeared about 240 million years ago, making them far older than any of the Australian dinosaurs we know of. These ancient ancestors weren't really too distinct from the species we're familiar with today – like the saltwater crocodile (*Crocodylus porosus*). The saltie is much younger than these ancestors, between 6 and 12 million years old, but its body hasn't **evolved** much from those first crocodilians.

The platypus has always been a bit of a mysterious creature. When European scientists first sent word of it back to England, people assumed it was a hoax! But the humble platypus has a **heritage** that goes back **aeons** – it has an ancestor, the *Steropodon galmani*, that was around 110 million years ago, during the Cretaceous era.

WATCH OUT! 3D

Scan this page to get a closer look at a snapping crocodile.

Activation: Unity Asset Store

Glossary

Aeons	The largest division of time, covering multiple eras and millions of years.
Bipedal	Two-legged.
Carnivorous	Meat-eating.
Conifers	A group of plants that flower all year and produce their seeds as cones, such as the pine, spruce or fir tree.
Evolved	Adapted from a previous generation.
Herbivorous	Plant-eating.
Heritage	A link to previous generations.
Predatory	Regularly preys upon other animals.
Protein	A molecule that is an essential part of all living things.
Quadrupedal	Four-legged.
Stockmen	Men who work on farms, especially with cattle.
Supercontinent	A great landmass that existed in the past, before being split into smaller landmasses known as continents.

DON'T FORGET!

You can also scan this page for even more hands-on fun. You can:

Create your own dinosaurs!

Take a picture with the dinos in our photobooth!

Learn how to pronounce their names!

Download wallpapers for your smartphone or tablet!